Last Shot Basketball

(A dramatic urban city basketball movie)

Lance Carsello

Dilema Music Productions, LTD

authorHOUSE®

AuthorHouse™
1663 Liberty Drive
Bloomington, IN 47403
www.authorhouse.com
Phone: 1-800-839-8640

First published by AuthorHouse 6/7/2010

ISBN: 978-1-4520-1063-2 (e)
ISBN: 978-1-4520-1064-9 (sc)

Library of Congress Control Number: 2010904942

Printed in the United States of America
Bloomington, Indiana

This book is printed on acid-free paper.

FADE IN:

SKYLINE VIEW OF MANHATTAN: NIGHT

MUSIC UP as **WE PAN** the Harlem area from central park to 155th St. polo grounds on to 8th Ave. **FOCUS** on a **GRAFITTI COVERED WALL** in the hood where a **YOUNG MAN** is spray painting "Three Deep" on the wall. Suddenly, a **HELICOPTER** appears behind him and its lights shine on him. He completes the last letter of "Three Deep" hurriedly and runs off into the projects. The spotlight from the helicopter illuminatesd the wall and "Three Deep".

DISSOLVE TO:

EXT. CRACKHOUSE: NIGHT

This is one of the crack houses operated by gang leader, **SNAP**. **DEE STRONG,** the leader of a rival gang and **MEMBERS** of his set are hiding in the bushes surrounding the house. They're loading their guns, as **SNOOPY,** one of Dee Strong's Boys, is on the porch about to knock on the door. He knocks loudly.

Dee Strong
Nigger, not so hard!

Snoopy
Sshh! Man, I got it!

He knocks again, this time lighter, and a **MAN** comes to the door and looks out through a peephole.

Man
Yeah?

Snoopy
(beaming, "craving crack")Hey man, can I get
one of them thangs?

Man
Let's see your money!

Snoopy reaches into his shirt pocket and takes out a twenty dollar bill. He puts it through the peephole for the man to see. Meanwhile, Dee Strong and the rest of the gang are prepared to raid the house. The man doesn't immediately open the door.

Snoopy
Come on man! I just want to get a twenty!

The man opens the door and Dee Strong and the others rush into the house, knocking the man down.

Dee Strong
(shooting into the air)
Freeze Niggas! Don't nobody move!

There are several people in the house. **A LADY** is standing at a stairway in the living room and tries to run up the stairs upon Dee Strong's gang raiding the house. He shoots over the lady's head.

> Dee Strong
> Wanda is that you? What the hell you
> doing in here?

She stops in her tracks and turns around slowly.

> Snoopy
> Look over there Dee! This motherfucker
> got all our customers!

> Dee Strong
> So all you motherfuckers gonna play me
> like this, huh! All you bitches owe me
> money! Dope feen hoes! Get y'alls
> fucking asses out here!

Several of the people start toward the door. **LOE,** one of Snap's gang members – a young man in his early twenties – head for the door and Dee Strong grabs him in the chest and shoves him against the wall placing a gun to his head.

> Dee Strong
> Where the hell you think you going, punk?

> Loe
> Nowhere man!

> Dee Strong
> That's right, no fucking where! Now
> where's the shit and the money? **(pressing
> the gun harder to Loe's head).** Where is
> if before I smoke your ass!

> Loe
> It's in the kitchen under the sink in a
> brown paper bag.

> Dee Strong
> Then let's get it!

Dee Strong drags Loe towards the kitchen, still holding the pistol to his head. The other gang members rush the crack heads out, taking whatever money they may have.

KITCHEN:

Dee Strong drags Loe into the kitchen and over to the sink. He pushes him down on the floor and he opens the cabinet door. There is a brown paper bag under the sink. Dee Strong removes the bag and inspects it. There's **SEVERAL BILLS** in the bag, as well as **CLEAR PLASTIC BAGS** containing crack. Dee Strong smiles as he thrills over his find. He stands with the bag in his hand and looks down at Loe.

                        Dee Strong
                Tell Snap I said thanks!

                          Loe
                He ain't gonna like this shit man.

Dee Strong shoots him in the leg. Loe screams.

                        Dee Strong
                Shut up bitch! You in the wrong
                place to be talking shit!

Dee Strong exits the kitchen with the bag.

LIVING ROOM:

Dee Strong enters the living room from the kitchen.

                        Dee Strong
                (to the gang members)
                Let's bail!

They all head for the door.

                                            CUT TO:

GYMANSIUM INT: NEXT DAY

The **MUSIC** continues from the previous scene and it is revealed that the music is actually the bouncing of a basketball. Four young men playing a game of "21". The young men are: **CHRIS COLLINS,** aka **"CREEM" 28; JEFF JAMISON,** aka **"FREEZ" 28; STEVEN STARLING,** aka **"SMOOV" 29** and **ALVIN ANDERSON,** aka **"SHORT CHANGE" 27.** Three of the boys are black. Creem is the product of an interracial marriage. Freez has the ball when the scene opens. He fakes Smoov and drives to the goal making the basket. Freez goes to the line and concentrates on making the shot. He shoots and misses and Short Change rebounds. They all converge on Short Change and in an effort to drive to the basket, he bumps Creem and screams in agony as though he's hurt. He's faking an injury. The other guys let their guards down and rush to his aid.

                          Creem
                You alright, Short?

                          Freez
                You alright nigga?

                      Short Change
                Damn motherfucker! Watch out!

                          Creem

Hey man! Get your little ass out the way!

> Smoov
> (to Creem and Freez)
> Man ain't nothing wrong with that fool!

Short Change limps toward Smoov as though he were about to confront him, still holding the basketball in his hand.

> Short Change
> (rushing towards the basket)
> You got that shit right!

Short Change lays the bail up and Smoov attempts to stop him. He makes the basket and turns to the guys and laughs. He raises his arms in victory.

> Short Change
> Twenty-one Hoes!

The other guys stand and look at each other momentarily.

> Freez
> (jokingly)
> Let's whip this nigga's ass!

Short Change runs towards the exit with the three guys close behind him.

CUT TO:

EXT. CREEM'S HOUSE: LATE EVENING

Creem lives in an affluent neighborhood on the upper East Side in a Brownstone. He drives a late model Jeep. He drives into the driveway. He gets out of the Jeep, with the basketball in hand, and enters the house.

INT. HOUSE:

Creem enters the living room and heads for the stairway, when his mother enters from another room. She's a sophisticated white lady

who resents her son hanging out with Freez and the others. His mother, **VICTORIA COLLINS,** stands staring at him. He stops at the bottom of the stairway.

> Victoria
> You were supposed to come directly home
> from school today!

> Creem
> I know, but something came up.

> Victoria
> What came up?

                    Creem
                Something!

Creem turns to walk up the stairs and Victoria hurries behind him. She grabs him by the arm and turns him to her.

                    Victoria
                You were with those boys again! Weren't
                you?

                    Creem
                Mom! Those are my friends! Just regular guys!
                Why can't I pick my own?
                friends? We're not doing anything wrong!

                    Victoria
                I don't approve of it, Chris! And neither does
                your father!

                    Creem
                You don't understand!

He turns and walks away.

                    Victoria
                What don't I understand? Chris, I'm talking
                to you!

He disappears down the hallway. She turns, disgusted, and walks down the stairs.

                                                        Cut to:

INT. FREEZ'S HOUSE: SAME EVENING

Freez's home is located in the heart of the ghetto, a neighborhood that's deteriorated because of drug trafficking in the area and gang violence and intervention. His home is furnished primarily with second hand furniture and the place isn't very clean. Freez enters the apartment and stops in the doorway, upon seeing his **MOTHER**, Nita Jamison, lying on the sofa drunk and asleep. He shakes his head in disgust and walks past her, knocking her arm out of his way. He walks on to his bedroom and opens the door and enters. The room is dark and he turns on the lights. Dee Strong, his older brother, is in the bottom **BUNKBED** asleep, with a fan blowing directly on him. He wakes up when the light comes on.

                    Dee Strong
                    (covering his head)
                Man, turn that damn light off!

                    Freez
                Nigga, I live here too! (Under his breath).
                Dumb motherfucker!

Freez walks over to the dresser and eases the top drawer open. He sees a **WAD OF MONEY** and is about to pick it up, when, without having to remove the cover,

> Dee Strong
> Put it back!

> Freez
> (turns startled)
> Man, I ain't got nothing!

> Dee Strong
> Yeah! Now put it back!

Dee Strong sits up in bed.

> Freez
> Dee, where all this money come from man?

> Dee Strong
> Let's just say, I cashed in on an investment!

Freez walks over to the bed and sits down.

> Freez
> Investment my ass! You've been…

> Dee Strong
> (interrupting)
> Wait nigga! What I tell you?

> Freez
> Alright man! Don't be so sensitive!
> It don't matter no how as long as you kick me
> down a few ends.

> Dee Strong
> (getting out of bed)
> Nigga, please!

Dee Strong walks over to the dresser and opens the drawer. Freez gets up and follows. He gazes at his money.

> Freez
> Man you know Mr. Eddie's having that three-on
> three basketball tournament and I need a new
> pair of gym shoes and a couple of fresh hook-
> ups. And, I gotta pay my part of the hundred
> dollar registration fee.

Dee Strong turns to Freez.

> Dee Strong

                    I just had the boosters bring you all kind of
                    shit!

                              Freez
                    Dee that was some weak ass shit!
                    Besides, that looks like some shit you'd wear!
                    Ha! Ha! Ha!

Dee Strong closes the drawer and walks back over to the bed and lies down. Freez
follows.

                              Freez
                    What you gonna do man! Come on Dee!
                    (sarcastically) Okay, what you want me to do?
                    Kiss your ass! You acting like Mom now! So
                    what... you want me to sing for my supper!

Dee Strong laughs and turns to Freez.

                              Dee Strong
                    Alright. Get five hundred and don't ask me for
                    shit else!

Freez walks over to the dresser and opens the drawer. He counts out six one-
hundred dollar bills.

                              Dee Strong
                    Nigga, I said five, not six!

                              Freez
                    Oh man, damn I thought you said six.

                              Dee Strong
                    Ain't shit wrong with your hearing.
                    You heard what I said!

Freez puts the money in his pocket and shuts the drawer. He walks toward the
door.

                              Freez
                    Yo, thanks for the ends, cuz. I gotta make a
                    run.

                              Dee Strong
                    Freez, you ain't living large like Creem's ass,
                    alright!

Freez starts out the door.

                              Dee Strong
                    And turn that fucking light off!

Freez turns the light out and closes the door behind him.

LIVINGROOM:

Freez enters the living room form the hallway. He walks over to the phone which sets on a small table. He sits in a chair across form the sofa, where his mother is still lying. He stares at her for a moment and then picks up the phone and dials. He waits for someone to answer. When Smoov answers…

> Freez
> Yo Smoov, buzz Creem and tell him we on for 125th tomorrow.

                                                                                      CUT TO:

SMOOV'S KITCHEN:

Smoov is from a middle-class family and the house is representative of such a family. Smoov is sitting at the counter talking to Freez on the phone.

> Smoov
> What-up dog. Dee must of kicked you down some funds.

INTERCUT PHONE CONVERSATION:

> Freez
> Yeah, he tightened me up.

> Smoov
> Cool! I think I got enough saved up and my ole man supposed to drop me some bucks too.

> Freez
> Don't worry. Your boy is full!
> Anyway, you know we ain't got nothing to worry about. Creem got that plastic money!

> Smoov
> Alright man. I'm gonna call Creem now.

> Freez
> You call Short Change too and tell him to have his ass ready on time for a change.

> Smoov
> Alright! Peace!

Smoov hangs up the phone and walks out of the kitchen into the living room. There are several pictures of his older brother and sister graduating on the wall. His **MOM, LOIS STARLING,** is sitting on the sofa reading her Bible. He walks up to her and gives her a kiss on the cheek.

>   Smoov
>   Good night Mom. Love you.

He walks toward his bedroom.

>   Lois
>   Steven, is Mr. Eddie having the tournament
>   this year?

>   Smoov
>   Yeah Mom. We register next week and we're
>   gonna take the championship too. (He gestures
>   as though he's shooting a basket-ball). Three
>   Deep strikes again.

>   **DISSOLVE TO:**

125th St. MALL: NEXT MORNING

Walking up street are Freez, Smoov, Creem and Short Change.

Walking the opposite way are **TWO YOUNG BLACK GIRLS**. As the girls pass, all four of the boys turn and stare at them.

>   Short Change
>   What's up ma, can I get them digits?

>   Freez
>   Yeah ma, give him your email, Facebook and
>   Twitter info.

>   Smoov
>   Just give that nigga an email address!

>   Creem
>   Then maybe his little short ass will sit down
>   somewhere!

The girls smile and blush as they continue to walk. Short Change is looking back at them when one of them turns and smiles at him.

>   Short Change
>   Hey, I'll catch y'all in a minute!

Short Change runs down the street after them. The other guys turn and are shocked at his actions.

>   Freez
>   That brother done lost his mind!

Short Change runs past the girls.

Short Change is at the end of the block waiting when the girls make it down. The guys have gone on.

>   Short Change
> What took you so long? (They smile and walk on and he follows) Damn ma, you got a body like Beyonce!

>   Girl #1
> Who are you talking to, me or her?

>   Short Change
> Of course ma, I'm talking to you!
> So! How about catching a movie tonight?

>   Girl #1
> I already have a date!

>   Short Change
>   (to the other girl)
> Then what about you Shorty?

>   Girl #2
> Well, Okay.

>   Short Change
> Cool! I'm glad you ain't trying to act stuck up like this bitch!

>   Girl #2
> Who you calling a bitch?

>   Girl #1
> I know you didn't call my friend no bitch!

>   Short Change
> Pshh chill! I'm sorry. Why don't you give me your phone number and I'll call you later?

>   Girl #2
> No you won't! Not after you done called my friend a bitch!

>   Short Change
>   (turning and walking away)
> Then fuck both of you bitches!

>   Girls
> Fuck you!

SEVERAL PEOPLE are stopping to watch the incident, as Short Change makes an obscene gesture as he walks away.

SHOE STORE:

Short Change walks into the shoe store where the other guys are examining the different brands of gym shoes exhibited on the wall. **A STORE EMPLOYEE** walks up to Short Change when he enters.

> Employee
> May I help you?

> Short Change
> No man! I'm with my boys!

Short Change walks up to the guys and Freez turns to him.

> Freez
> Where the hoes sick nigga?

> Short Change
> I copped fool! I got both them hoes numbers!

> Creem
> (extending his portable phone to Short Change)
> So you got it like that huhn! Here's the phone! Call 'em then?

> Short Change
> Yeah right nigga! Like this is Star Trek, they done made it home in warp fucking speed!

> Creem
> You can call and see if they gave you a 'legit' number!

> Short Change
> Man, I ain't going through all that shit! And what's taking you niggas so long! You acting like a bunch of bitches in the bathroom!

> Smoov
> (holding up a tennis shoe)
> Nigga this is what's taking so long! You see that sole! Read that nigga! You know what that says! Air Jordan! (he opens a pamphlet which is attached to the shoe.) Read that! The stretch lace pocket allows you to secure your laces and keep them out of the way, during intensive play! And, the two Nike air cushioning units provide out-standing cushioning throughout the life of this here shoe! Do you get it nigga! Air Jordan, punk!

> Creem

(holding up another brand)
Fuck that! Fuck Air Jordan! You see this here!
This is the new G-Unit by Reebok! 50 Cent is
getting paid because this shit is hot.

Freez
Man, both of you niggas don't know shit!
Before there was Reebok and Air Jordan's
there was these bad motherfuckers... All Stars
by Converse! These shoes and motherfuckers
like Earl the Pearl Monroe and Clyde Frazier
revolutionized the game go basketball!

Short Change
All you niggas talking this bullshit, but I don't
fuck with nothing unless it says S. Carter! And
you know why? Cause that Nigga Jay Z is the
shit!

The store employee walks up to the boys.

Employee
Can I help you brothers?

Smoov
Yeah! Hold up! (to the others) Man we can't be
fooling around with all these different brands.
We got to be down with the same shoe in the
tournament!

Creem
Look here! Y'all bust out the Le Bron James
Nikes and I'll sport the funds. But you got to
buy your own motherfucking hookups to go
with em!

Freez
Hell yeah!

Smoov
Bet!

Short Change
Oh! Since I ain't playing, fuck me huhn?

Creem
Na! Na! I ain't forgot about you! (to the employee)
Give the lil nigga some socks.

The others laugh including the employee.

> Creem (cont)
> I'm just bullshitting! Hook us up man!

They all tell the employee their sizes and he goes to the back to get the shoes.

AT THE REGISTER:

The employee has gotten the shoes and is about to ring the purchase up. The boys are standing at the register.

> Employee
> Will this be cash or charge?

> Creem
> Charge! (he opens his wallet and displays a **NUMBER OF CREDIT CARDS**. He hands the employee his **VISA** and the employee rings up the purchase and bags the shoes separately.)

They each get their bags and turn and exit the store, laughing and talking on their way out.

CUT TO:

GYMNASIUM: AFTERNOON

Freez, Smoov, Creem and Short change are in the gym. Freez is standing center court and Short Change is sitting next to him. Smoov is defensively guarding Creem as he dribbles toward the basket. Smoov steals the ball from Creem and makes a jumper.

> Short Change
> Half breed, if that's the best you can do, then you can sit your ass down right here!

> Creem
> Nigga, fuck you!

> Short Change
> Yeah, it'll be the best fuck you ever had!

> Freez
> Short Change, shut the hell up! Ain't nobody got time to listen to you shit! The tournament, is in two days!

> Short Change
> That's all I'm saying nigga that's all I'm saying!

Smoov has gotten the ball and tosses it in to Creem.

> Smoov
> Come on man! Let's go again!

Creem cuts his eyes at Short Change.

> Short Change
> What up Gee? What you peeping me for? You
> better keep you eyes on the damn ball.

> Freez
> (grabbing Short Change)
> I told you to shut up!

> Short Change
> Alright! Alright!

Freez lets him go and Creem starts to dribble toward the basket with Smoov still guarding him. This time Creem manages to make a drive to the basket and scores.

> Creem
> You've got so much mouth, let's see what you
> can do!

Short Change takes the ball and stands up. He starts to dribble the ball, walking slowly toward Creem who is moving to guard him. Smoov walks toward Short Change to guard him also.

> Short Change
> Sit your ass down Smoov! Let me show this half
> breed something!

> Creem
> Let me stick him Smoov so I can shut his fucking
> mouth up!

Smoov moves out of the playing are and stands next to Freez.

> Freez
> Creem fixin' to "D" his ass up!

Short Change starts to make his drive to the basket, but Creem is doing an exceptional job of guarding him. Short Change turns and dribbles back toward the half court line.

> Smoov
> What's the matter? Can't hang?

> Short Change
> Strategy dude! Strategy! But, from watching
> you play, you wouldn't know what that is!

As Short Change is talking to Smoov, Creem steals the ball from him. Creem dribbles to the basket and lays the ball up.

                              Creem
                         (to Short Change)
                      I like your strategy!

Freez and Smoov laugh.

                          Short Change
                           (to Creem)
                        Give me the ball!

Creem throws him the ball and Short Change starts toward the goal with Creem guarding him!

                          Short Change
                   I'm about to school your ass, gee!

                              Creem
                              Yeah?

                          Short Change
                              Yeah!

Short Change fakes and attempts a jumper, only to have Creem smack it in his face. Freez and Smoov laugh hilariously.

                          Short Change
                 Damn man! You fouled the hell out of me!

                              Creem
                           Foul my ass!

                              Freez
                     That man ain't fouled you!

                              Smoov
                   He just put that shit back in your face!

                          Short Change
                   Both of y'all go to hell! I know when a
                   motherfucker done fouled me!

Creem picks up the ball and hands it to Short Change.

                              Creem
                   Alright, I fouled you! Here stop crying! Try it
                   again, Homey!

                          Short Change
                   (knocking the ball out of Creem's hand)You
                   kiss my ass!

Freez and Smoov walk up to Creem and Short Change. Freez puts his arm around Short Change.

> Freez
> Ain't life a bitch?

> Short Change
> Fuck you!

They all walk toward the gym door.

EXT. GYMNASIUM:

The four guys exit the gym, with Creem carrying the basketball.

> Creem
> So what you got up?

> Smoov
> I'm about to jet to the crib! I got somethings to
> take care of.

> Short Change
> You always got some kinda shit to do at home!

> Smoov
> Maybe you would too, if your old man would
> let you come home!

Freez and Smoov laugh.

CUT TO:

HARLEM RUCKERS PARK: MORNING

The Park is located in Harlem across from the Polo grounds projects and it is packed with teenagers and adults who have come to see some of the states best basketball players compete in the highly regarded, "Rucker's 3 on 3 Street Basketball Tournament". **PAN** the park where a few **POLICE CARS** are cruising through and come to **FOCUS** on Creem driving up in his Jeep, with the top off. He's driving slowly as he talks on his cell phone. **MUSIC** is blasting from his stereo sound system, as he dials another number. He starts to park as he awaits an answer. Freez, Smoov and Short Change walk up behind him and Freez taps him on the shoulder as he hangs the phone up. Simultaneously, Short Change's **IPhone** starts ringing. Creem turns around, as Short Change checks his **IPhone**.

> Freez
> Where you been man?

> Creem
> I had to run some documents to my mother at
> the office.

> Freez

Damn! We thought you forgot or some shit!

> Creem
> Yeah, right! Like I'm going to forget about the
> biggest basketball tournament in New York!

> Smoov
> If we don't get over there and sign in, we might
> have to forget about it!

Creem removes his IPod from the dash board and locks it in a secret compartment.

> Freez
> Man, hurry your ass up!

> Creem
> Chill out! I'm coming!

Creem gets out of the Jeep and turns the alarm on. He trots off to catch up with the others.

REGISTRATION TABLE:

The four young men walk up to the registration table where a middle-aged **MAN** and two **OTHERS** are signing teams in. The Three Deep team are dressed alike. Smoov steps up to the table and signs them in. Short Change pulls Creem to the side as Smoov signs them in and Freez watches Smoov.

> Creem
> What?

> Short Change
> Hey dog, look over there. I think we can make
> so quick money.

> Creem
> I want half this time!

> Short Change
> (hunching his shoulders) No problem, cuz!

Creem walks over onto the court and picks up a ball and begins shooting. There are a few other guys on the courts. Short Change walks over to the stands where a group of guys is sitting and sits down beside them. Creem is purposely missing.

> Boy in Stands
> (viewing Creem)
> Man, that half breed needs to sit his ass
> down.

> Short Change
> (to boy in stands)

I think the boy just needs to warm up a little
bit.

> Boy in Stands
Man, that half breed can't shoot!

> Short Change
I think he can hit one!

> Boy in Stands
That fool can't hit shit!

> Short Change
I got ten say he'll hit the next shot!

> Boy in Stands
Bet that shot!

> Short Change
> (to Creem)
Hey man, why don't you try that shot again!

> Creem
Who me?

> Short Change
Yeah you!

Creem attempts the jumper again and misses.

> Boy in Stands
Pay up!

Short Change hands him a ten dollar bill.

> Boy in Stands
You got another ten spot you wanna lose?

> Short Change
Aah shit. I guess so.

Short Change gives a sly not to Creem to miss again. Creem shoots and misses.
Short Change turns and hands the guy another ten dollar bill. The boy stands to
leave.

> Boy in Stands
Thanks for the easy twenty.

> Short Change
Wait a minute! I got fifty dollars says he makes
this shot!

> Boy in Stands

Man, you on!

                    Short Change
          Alright! (He goes in his pocket and takes fifty
          dollars out. He gives a sly nod to Creem to
          make the shot.)

Creem shoots a jumper from twenty four feet away and makes it.

                    Short Change
          Must be Murphy's Law!

Short Change extends his hand and the boy places fifty dollars in his hand. At that
moment, MR. EDDIE, a middle-age man who oversees the park and officiates the
tournament walks up. He stares at Short Change for a moment.

                    Short Change
                    (playing it off)
          Thanks for the loan! I'll pay you back!

                    Mr. Eddie
          Alvin! What did I tell you about gambling in
          my park boy! (Turning and yelling at Creem)
          Chris get your butt over here!

Creem walks up.

                    Mr. Eddie
          You guys are determined to mess up a good
          thing aren't you! I've told you before and I'm
          going to tell you again this park and everything
          in it belongs to me. That includes your two
          young asses while you're in it!

                    Mr. Eddie (cont.)
          That means no gambling, no gang banging no
          problems! I've dedicated my life to helping
          you young brothers build something positive
          for yourselves. Now, I've got sponsors, college
          administrators and even pro scouts attending
          these games and I'm not about to let you two
          bone heads screw it up for everyone else! So
          if I so much as hear about you guys doing this
          shit again, you're out of here! You got that!

Creem and Short Change both nod their heads yes. Mr. Eddie turns and walks
away.

                    Boy in Stands
          Man, give me my money back!

                    Short Change

> Man fuck you! You sure didn't mind taking my motherfucking money!

Short Change sticks his hand down into his pants as if he's got a gun.

CUT TO:

In another part of the park and in the passing, Smoov and Freez stop and talk to Mr. Eddie.

> Smoov
> What's happening Mr. Eddie?

> Mr. Eddie
> I'll tell you what's happening, you're two homeboys over there running that Murphy business again. Now, I've told them if I catch them again, they're out of here for good!

> Freez
> Don't worry Mr. Eddie, we'll make sure it won't happen again.

> Mr. Eddie
> Alright! Be cool!

Freez and Smoov walk up to Creem and Short Change.

> Freez
> (angrily)
> Man, I told y'all about that shit! You gonna really fuck up and get us thrown out of this tournament.

> Freez (cont)
> We almost pulled it off last year man! (to Creem) I ain't living large like you dude! I ain't got no rich momma and daddy who can send me to college and shit, so this is where I got to get mine!

Freez turns and walks away mumbling to himself, as the others look on.

BASKETBALL COURT: LATER

The tournament has begun and **THE SYNDICATE BOYS** are playing another team. Mr. Eddie is officiating the game. The Syndicate Boys are one of the favored teams to win. They are totally dominating their opponents (**THE GAMES ARE TO BE CHOREOGRAPHED**). The members of Three Deep, along with Short Change, sit and watch the game. They are closely examining the playing skills of The Syndicate Boys.

Creem
(referring to a syndicate player)
That kid got game!

Freez
No problem, I can handle him!

The Syndicate Boys continue playing and eventually win the game 85-52. **THE WINNERS BOARD** shows the Syndicate Boys moving up.

BASKETBALL COURT: LATER

Three Deep is taking the court against their **OPPONENTS.** Three Deep is the favored team. Short Change is on the sidelines. The **WHISTLE** blows and the game is underway.

Short Change
Alright, now you really getting' ready to see some niggas play some serious ball. (He motivates the crowd into chanting "Three Deep")

The crowd responds immediately when Freez throws down a spectacular two hand, reverse, in your face slam dunk. Freez is the tough alley ball player who specializes in coming down the lane. Smoov is the ball handling type player similar to "Allen Iverson", and Creem is the three point king and outside shooter. **(THE GAME IS CHOREOGRAPHED)** With seconds left in the game, Smoov dishes a sweet wrap around, no-look pass to Creem who buries an all net jumper deep from the corner to end their victorious lopsided game. Short Change is the first person to run onto the court to congratulate the team, followed by several of their friends. The **WINNERS BOARD** show Three Deep moving up. Near the winners board is Dee Strong and several members of his gang. Dee Strong flashes a few signs to Freez to congratulate him. Mr. Eddie has noticed the gang members and walks over to Freez.

Mr. Eddie
(pulling Freez to the side)
You see that tall guy over there with the glasses on?

Freez
(finally sees the guy)
Yeah. I see him.

Mr. Eddie
He's a scout from St. Johns, and he's here to see basketball players and basketball games, not gangsters and gang-banging. So, tell your brother this ain't Dodge City!

Freez

> Mr. Eddie, you know they respect you. Ain't gonna be no stuff.

                    Mr. Eddie
You just make sure, or I will!

Smoov, Creem and Short Change walk over to Mr. Eddie and Freez.

                    Creem
Mr. Eddie, we apologize for what we did earlier.

                    Mr. Eddie
Stay out of trouble! I'll see you at your next game.

Mr. Eddie walks away and the boys walk off. FOLLOW as they walk toward Creem's jeep.

                    Freez
Mr. Eddie wiggin' about Dee and his boys.

                    Smoov
Well man, you can't blame him, they look like they ready to start something at all times.

                    Freez
He just comes to cheer the nigga on.

                    Short Change
But Free, you got to admit, Dee is a ruthless motherfucker!

                    Freez
Short, ain't nobody asked your worthless ass shit! So shut the fuck up!

They continue toward the jeep.

                                                  CUT TO:

INT. BUILDING: THAT NIGHT

A party is taking place and **SEVERAL PEOPLE** are dancing in the center of the floor. **OTHERS** are standing around. Freez, Smoov, Creem and Short Change are talking with a few of their **BOYS**. A **GUY** is a well known Disc Jockey.

                    Smoov
The team we got to watch is the Syndicate Boyz.

                    Short Change
Man, they ain't shit!

Freez
How the hell you know? Your little short ass
don't know jack about basketball!

Boy #1
So when's your next game?

Smoov
Tomorrow at 1:30.

A beautiful, young girl, **NIKKI** approaches them with a couple of her **GIRLFRIENDS**.
She's staring at Creem as she walks up.

Nikki
I saw you guys play today. You're really
smooth.

Smoov
(stepping forward)
That's me!

Nikki
Excuse me.

Smoov
That's my name...Smoov!

Nikki
Oh, that's cute. Who's your friend? (referring
to Creem)

Smoov
Who him? Half Breed?

Nikki
Oh, he's mulato?

Girlfriend #1
Honey, he ain't mixed the way he was shooting
that ball today!

Creem
Let's just say I'm a little bit of Italian, Puerto
Rican, and black.

Nikki
Well, excuse me.

Freez
You're excused baby, right to the dance floor.

Freez takes her by the hand, as a popular 50 Cent song plays, and leads her to the dance floor. Smoov and Short Change lead the other two girls to the dance floor. **FOLLOW** Freez and Nikki. As they're dancing Nikki is still watching Creem.

> Freez
> Look. What I'm saying ain't no game. Get with
> me and you can't lose!

> Nikki
> Are you sure about that?

> Freez
> Positive ma!

They continue to dance.

> Nikki
> (whispering in his ear)
> 555-5089, now if you can't remember that, then
> you can't hang.

> Freez
> (gesturing a jumper)
> Then count it. I'll call you later.

They continue to dance. She is still watching Creem, who notices and turns away after a moment.

EXT BUILDING WHERE PARTY IS GOING ON: SAME NIGHT

There are **SEVERAL CARS** parked along the street and **SEVERAL PEOPLE** standing around the cars and along the street. Freez, Smoov, Creem and Short Change exit the building. Short Change is drunk. He's in front of the others and he's shaking some dice in his hand.

> Short Change
> Six, eight. Seven, eleven. Paying all craps.
> Bet you can't throw over seven nigga!

> Smoov
> Give me them damn dice!

> Short Change
> I ain't givin' you shit! I'm grown!

> Smoov
> You're drunk! And we ain't getting in no fights
> tonight!

They walk toward the jeep. They get in the jeep and Creem turns on the music.

> Short Change

Hey, give me the phone. I gotta call Shorty who
I met at the mall.

                    Creem
(handing him the phone) Don't tie my line up
long. I got a call to make in a minute.

Short Change takes the phone and dials a number. He waits for the party to
answer.

                Short Change
Hey baby, I'm tied up right now. But I'm going
to get with you a little later.

Freez, who is sitting in the back with Short Change notices that he has receiver
down.

                    Freez
Yeah! Much later! Give me that damn phone!
You ain't talkin' to nobody!

Freez snatches the phone from Short Change!

                    Freez
Man, this nigga back here bullshittin' on your
phone. (he hands the phone to Creem).

Nikki and her girlfriends walk up and stop at the jeep.

                    Nikki
We locked our keys in the car. Can you use
your phone to call a tow truck?

                Short Change
You don't need no tow truck. Let Freez thieving
ass unlock it for you!

                    Freez
Shut up nigga! (to Nikki) I think I can help you.
(to Short Change) I ain't no thief punk!

Freez, Smoov and Short Change get out of the jeep and follow the girls to their car
which isn't far from the jeep. Creem makes a phone call and sits in the jeep talking.
Freez starts working to unlock the door. Short Change and Smoov are talking to
Nikki's girlfriends. Smoov is holding a lighter size light for Freez to see by. As he's
talking to the girl he's moving the light.

                    Freez
Man, shine the damn light where I can see! (He
continues to work on the door.)

Nikki sees Creem talking on the phone and walks back to the Jeep.

Nikki

I never got your name.

Creem

My name is Creem.

Nikki

Creem. I like that. It's different. Who you talking to on the phone?

Creem

To my girlfriend.

Nikki

Maybe I should leave.

Creem

That's not a bad idea.

She turns and walks back to her car and up to Freez. He turns to her.

Freez

So, ma you don't think I can handle 555-5089?

Nikki

We'll see!

Freez

We sure will!

He unlocks the door and opens it for her.

Nikki

Thank you. (She starts to get in the car.) Oh, guess what. I just remembered, I had another set of keys in my purse. (She dangles the keys in front of Freez.)

Freez starts to say something nasty, but stops.

Freez turns to walk toward the jeep, when suddenly a **CAR** comes around the corner speeding. The **GUYS** inside the car are yelling and hanging out the window.

GUYS IN CAR

ONEWAY NINES! ONEWAY NINES! (They continue)

Short Change and Smoov turn and hurry toward the jeep, along with Freez. Creem hangs up the phone and cranks up the jeep. Nikki and her friends peel off. SEVERAL of the KIDS scramble to leave. SEVERAL CARS peal away from the curbs. The guys get in the jeep and Creem starts to pull away. The car blocks Creem's path and SNAP, the leader of the gang, stares at Freez. Freez stares back at him. Snap points a pistol at Freez and it is fixed on him momentarily. Snap laughs and they pull away. Freez stares at the car as if drives away and the others stare at him.

CUT TO:

INT.   CREEM'S HOUSE, UPPER EAST SIDE BROWNSTONE: NEXT MORNING

Creem comes down the stairs with his basketball gear and heads for the door. His mother, who's in the dining room, calls for him. He turns and walks into the dining room. She's eating breakfast.

> Victoria
> Good morning.

> Creem
> Morning mom.

> Victoria
> I hope you haven't made any plans for today. Your father and I want to spend some time with you.

> Creem
> I'm sorry Mom, but I'm playing in a basketball tournament today.

> Victoria
> So, are you saying this basketball tournament is more important than your father and I?

> Creem
> Mom. Please don't start that today!

> Victoria
> I'm not starting anything! I asked a simple question. Is this basketball tournament more important than your family?

> Creem
> (turning to leave)
> I'll see you later Mom.

Victoria gets up and follow him toward the door.

> Victoria
> Chris, I forbid you to leave this house!

> Creem

> Mom, we've practiced all year for this tournament and I have an obligation to be there!

He opens the door to exit as his father, JONATHAN, is coming in from his morning jog. He stops at the door.

> Jonathan
> What's going on here?

> Victoria
> I've instructed Chris not to leave this house and he's defying me!

> Creem
> Dad, I'm playing in a basketball tournament! We won yesterday and we have another game today!

> Victoria
> I don't care about your little tournament! I want you to spend more time with me and your father!

> Creem
> I got to go! I don't have time for this!

He walks out the door pass his father, who turns to him.

> Jonathan
> Chris!

> Creem
> Dad, I got to go!

> Jonathan
> I think you should reconsider. Now!

Creem gets in the jeep and drives as his mother and father look on in disappointment.

CUT TO:

HARLEM RUCKERS PARK: SAME DAY

The park is crowded and a game is being played. Freez, Smoov, Creem and Short Change are walking toward the court area.

> Short Change
> (to Freez)
> Did you tell Dee what happened, dude?

> Freez

Man, ice that! Ain't no thang!

                    Short Change
I told him. Fuck that! That nigga coulda
popped you!

                    Freez
Look man, I ain't got nothing to do with that!
That's them fools out there slangin' and
bangin'

                    Creem
Freez, you got to admit that was a scary situation
bro.

                    Freez
I ain't scared of no gat! And I ain't scared of
nobody caring a gat either! But I'll tell you
what, he better not fuck with my brother!

                    Creem
Yeah man.

                    Smoov
Let's break to the court.

They walk on.

COURTSIDE:

Freez, Smoov and Creem are strapping up (putting on arm bands, knee pads, etc.)
MUSIC up / "Three Deep" (New York theme song) by Jay Z. and Alicia Keys.

COURT: INTERCUT

MUSIC continues as Three Deep dominates their opponent and the Syndicate Boyz
dominate their opponent.

PARKING LOT AT PARK:

Three Deep and Short Change are walking toward their car, when the members of
the Syndicate Boyz drive by slowly in front of them.

                    Short Change
Y'all hoes ain't shit!

                    Smoov
                 (to Short Change)
Man be cool!

                    Short Change
Them punk asses think they the shit cause they
won last year! Fuck them! The only reason
they won is because Freez pulled up hurt. (to

the boys in the car) Y'all gonna have to come deffer this year hoes!

The boys stop the car and get out.

> Player #1
> Shut your punk as up or I'll fuck you up!

> Freez
> Excuse me! I think y'all better get the fuck on! Before…

Mr. Eddie is walking toward his car when he notices the boys. He turns to them.

> Mr. Eddie
> Is there a problem here?

> Smoov
> No sir, we just rappin' about basketball!

> Mr. Eddie
> Well, the games are over fellas. I suggest you young brothers go home and get some rest! The games are getting tougher now. (he walks on)

> Player #2
> Yeah, much tougher! You sissies try to get with this (he pats his chest) and it's void!

> Short Change
> Come game time you motherfuckers gonna get dissed in the conflict!

> Player #1
> We'll see!

The Syndicate Boyz get back in the car and drive off.

> Creem
> Short Change, sometimes you talk too damn much!

> Short Change
> What! You scared of them motherfuckers or something'.

> Creem
> No. The only thing I'm scared of is that I might have to whip your ass!

> Short Change

> (laughingly)
> Yeah! I'll knock your dick in the dirt!

They continue walking

CUT TO:

SMOOV'S HOUSE: THAT EVENING

Smoov and his family are eating dinner. His mother and **FATHER** are at the head of the table and his tree sisters and three brothers are seated too.

> Mr. Starling
> Sorry, I couldn't make it to your game today, Steve. They got me working overtime all this week. We need the money. How did it go?

> Smoov
> We won.

> Mrs. Starling
> When's your next game?

> Smoov
> We're scheduled to play this other team called The Syndicate Boyz next Saturday morning.

> Mr. Starling
> Aren't they the team that won it last year?

> Smoov
> Yeah pop! But not this year!

> Sister #1
> Steve I wanna go to your game!

> Mrs. Starling
> What time does the game start?

> Smoov
> 10 a.m.

> Mr. Starling
> (to his wife and kids)
> I think we can make it.

They continue eating.

DISSOLVE TO:

SMOOV'S BEDROOM:

Smoov is working out, lifting weights, as he listens to music. His father walks in and Smoov sits up on the bench and his father sits on the bed.

> Mr. Starling
> Your mother tells me that you got some important mail today.

> Smoov
> Yeah, but it's no big deal, Pop.

> Mr. Starling
> Tell me about it.

> Smoov
> I thought Mom would tell you.

> Mr. Starling
> No. She wanted you to be the person to tell me.

Smoov gets up and walks over to the stereo and turns it down. He takes an envelope off of the dresser and walks over and hands it to his father. Smoov sits down on the bench and stares at his father as he takes the letter from the envelope and reads it. He looks up from the letter and smiles.

> Mr. Starling
> Congratulation! I'm proud of you son!

Smoov smiles.

CUT TO:

CREEM'S HOUSE: SAME NIGHT

Creem and his mother and father are sitting in the dining room eating dinner. They are questioning him about his choice of friends.

> Jonathan
> Chris, I have no problem with your playing basketball.

> Victoria
> Well, I do!

> Creem
> Mother it's not the basketball playing that bothers you. You don't like my friends!

> Victoria
> It's not that I don't like them. I don't like the influence they have on you!

> Creem

That's what I don't understand! What influence!
I'm my own person! I make my own decisions!
Nobody makes me do anything!

Jonathan

You better watch your tone of voice! You don't
speak to your mother like that!

Creem starts to get up from the table.

Jonathan

Sit down!

Creem

I'm finished eating!

Jonathan

I don't care! Sit down!

Creem sits down.

Jonathan

Chris, I've tried to be as open about this matter
as possible. And, so has your mother! But
you've put us in a terrible predicament! You're
a 28 year old senior this year and you should
be focusing on your plans for the future.

Creem

Dad, I already know what I'm going to do! And
I'm going to be a lawyer, just like you! You
and Mom decided all of that for me! The only
thing that I've ever asked is that you let me
play basketball! Now, you're telling me I can't
do that!

Victoria

Chris, we don't have a problem with you playing
basketball! It's who you play with and where
you play at that's the problem! How come you
don't play here in the area? There are plenty
of courts on the Upper East side.

Creem

Mom, I want to play where the nigga's be
ballin'.

Jonathan

How dare you use that vernacular in this
house!

> Creem
> I'm sorry. I want to play where the competition
> level is at an all time high!

Victoria is shocked at her son's statement and sits shaking her head in disgust.

> Creem
> Mom, try to understand. All I want to do is play
> basketball with some guys I like. They're okay
> guys.

> Jonathan
> Excuse yourself, Chris.

Creem looks up at his father and gets up and walks away from the table. They're both disgusted.

CUT TO:

FREEZ'S HOUSE:

Freez enters the house and goes directly to the bathroom and washes his hands. He then goes to the kitchen to eat dinner. He finds the sink full of dirty dishes and two pots on the stove with food in them that has soured. He gets angry, but tries to conceal it. He opens the refrigerator and finds it empty. He turns in disgust and walks into the living room, and meets his mother and a **MAN FRIEND** staggering out of her bedroom. They're both drunk. He stops in his tracks and stares at them. His mother stops momentarily, half-sobering up, and stares back at him.

> Freez
> Who's he?

> Nita
> A friend!

> Freez
> Get him out of here!

> Man
> (to Nita)
> Hey, I'll see you later!

> Freez
> Yeah! Much later!

> Nita
> (talking to the man)
> You ain't got to go baby! I'm the one who runs
> this house!

> Man

No, I'm going to go!

The man starts toward the door and Nita rushes and grabs him by the arm.

>   Nita
> This here is my house and you ain't got to go
> nowhere until I say go!

>   Freez
> Well, he better get the fuck outta here!

>   Man
> She say I ain't got to go no mother-fuckin'
> where!

Freez runs into his bedroom and **WE FOLLOW**. He gets one of Dee's GUNS from the back of the closet and rushes back into the living room. Freez runs up to the man an puts the gun to his head. His mother starts screaming. Freez cocks the trigger gritting his teeth. We SEE the man pants, in the groin area reveal a small wet spot that rapidly spreads.

>   Freez
>   (glancing down)
> You got to go to the bathroom!

The man nervously moves toward the door with Freez following, continuing to harass him with the gun firmly at his head. Nita continues screaming. The man opens the door and hurries out. Freez slams the door shut and turns to his mother.

>   Freez
> I'm sick of this bullshit! Momma, when are you
> gonna stop fucking up?

>   Nita
>   (walking up to him)
> Let me tell you one thing boy! I'm your momma,
> you ain't mine! And this is my house! You don't
> tell me shit, about who I can have here!

>   Freez
> I know who's house this is! But, damn! That's
> the fourth guy this week! Look at this damn
> kitchen, shit every-where! You ain't even put
> the food up from yesterday! How come you
> can't be like Smoov's mom? Even Creem's
> mother cares about him! Shit! Why can't you
> be a parent some damn times!

She slaps him. He turns and runs out the door with the gun in his hand.

EXT. BUILDING: SAME NIGHT

Freez runs out of the house and gets in his car. His mother runs after them yelling for him to come back. He drives away.

STREETS OF HARLEM. IN HIS NEIGHBORHOOD:

FOLLOW Freez as he drives aimlessly through the streets. **MUSIC** up. Freez is watching and studying the terrible conditions of the streets and area he lives in.

CUT TO:

INT. LIQUOR STORE: SAME NIGHT

Dee Strong and two of his gang members are at the counter purchasing beer. The cashier has rang the purchase up.

> Cashier
> That'll be $6.29.

Dee Strong hands him a five dollar bill and turns to one of his gang friends flaunting a roll of big bills.

> Dee Strong
> Hey man, I ain't got nothin' but large bills, give
> me two dollars.

The guy goes in his pocket and takes out two dollars. He hands them to the cashier and they exit with the beer.

EXT/ LIQUOR STORE:

Dee strong and his two boys walk out of the store, with one of the guys carrying the bag. There are a **FEW DRUNKS** and **DRUG-ADDICTS** hanging around the outside of the store. As they exit, Snap and **FOUR** of his boys attack them. One of the guys stabs Dee Strong in the arm before he can get his pistol out. The gun falls to the ground during their scuffle. Within seconds the **POLICE** arrive and they flee in different directions.

> Snap
> (to his gang)
> I want Dee Strong! Get that mother-fucker!

Dee Strong runs and Snap and his boys continue behind him. **FOLLOW** Dee Strong as he tries to get away from Snap.

INTERCUT:

NEARBY STREET:

Freez is still driving around. **A HELICOPTER'S SPOTLIGHT** shines on him.

ALLEY:

Dee Strong is running and they're behind him. Snap pulls a pistol and shoots at Dee Strong, but misses. Dee Strong jumps a fence and continues running with them closing.

NEXT STREET OVER:

Freez drives up to the intersection and stops at the red light. He's looking ahead when he sees Dee Strong run across the road on the other side of the intersection. He sees Snap and the gang running behind him. He runs the red light, almost getting into a wreck and drives up beside Dee Strong.

>   Freez
>   Get in!

Dee Strong gets in the car and as they're pulling off...

>   Dee Strong
>   I lost my fucking gun!

>   Freez
>   Here! I got the other one!

Dee Strong grabs the gun out of the seat and hangs out the window and shoots back toward Snap and his boys. He shoots one of the boys. They speed off. Freez is nervous and becomes more nervous when he sees Dee Strong bleeding.

>   Freez
>   Awe shit Man! You bleedin'!

>   Dee Strong
>   That motherfucker cut me!

>   Freez
>   I'm taking you to Bellevue!

Dee Strong grimaces in pain.

>   Dee Strong
>   You can't take me to a hospital! They got
>   warrants out on my ass!

>   Freez
>   You gotta go man! You bleedin' bad!

>   Dee Strong
>   (gritting his teeth)
>   I ain't going to no hospital Freez!

>   Freez
>   Then what man! What you want me to do? You
>   want me to take you to the house?

>   Dee Strong
>   No! They'll be looking for me there!

>   Freez

>   Wait a minute, I know! We can go to Nikki's
>   pad!

>   Dee Strong
>   Who the hell is Nikki?

>   Freez
>   Don't worry she's cool man!

They drive on.

CUT TO:

EXT. NIKKI'S APARTMENT:

Freez and Dee Strong are at the door and Nikki's opening the door. She's shocked when she sees Dee Strong.

>   Nikki
>   What took you so long?

>   Freez
>   Damn that! Get me a towel!

>   Nikki
>   Nigga you just met me! You better chill on
>   them orders! My name ain't Hazel!

Finally she sees Dee Strong bleeding.

>   Nikki
>   What happened?

>   Freez
>   My brother, he's hurt! We need help!

>   Nikki
>   My moms a nurse!

>   Freez
>   She is? Call her!

Nikki picks up the phone and calls her mother. We **HEAR** her in the **BACKGROUND** talking.

>   Freez
>   (to Dee Strong)
>   Dee, my girl's moms a nurse. She's gonna hook
>   you up.

Hours later we **SEE** Dee Strong lying comfortably on the sofa with his arm and shoulder bandaged up. He is sleep.

NIKKI'S BEDROOM: LATER

Nikki and Freez are engaged in sex.

CUT TO:

NEARBY PARK: EARLY NEXT MORNING

Freez and Dee Strong are in the car, driving by a nearby park. Freez pulls to the side and into the park. He stops the car.

>   Dee Strong
> Man, what you stoppin' for?

>   Freez
> Because you haven't heard shit I said!

>   Dee Strong
> Man, I ain't got time to hear you preach to me!
> Damn my shoulders killing me!

>   Freez
> Dee, you're my older brother and I respect
> you! But now it's time you listen to me! Snap's
> crew, tearing this town up looking for your ass!
> Your crew is ready to retaliate! When is the
> shit gonna stop? You got a gang of money now.
> What more you want? How much more do you
> need?

>   Dee Strong
> I want it all!

>   Freez
> Nobody gots it all, but God! And you ain't God!
> Though you might think you is! Damn man,
> you know Momma's on that shit! Why don't you
> take some of that money and put her in Rehab!
> Man, I need my mother and my brother. I can't
> take this shit no more man. I can't take it.

>   Dee Strong
> Man, I'm locked in you see. Ain't no get out
> other than a pine box. The world's a cruel
> place. Besides this is what I do best! As far
> as Momma's concerned, she still in love with
> Daddy, the motherfucker who left her for
> another bitch! Freez, I never was a child. I
> did my first stick up when I was nine! Sold my
> first rock when I was twelve! Blasted a nigga
> when I was fifteen! So, don't act like I don't
> know what pressure is! Cause I do! Now with
> you it's a different story. You gotta talent that

can take you some where. All I got is this (he pulls a pistol from his pants) and a record! And it ain't no hit!

DISSOLVE TO:

HARLEM RUCKERS PARK: LATER THAT MORNING

The park is crowded and a game is being played. **PAN** the park to SEE Smoov's family seated in the stands. Smoov, Creem and Short Change are down at the sidelines.

Smoov
(to Short Change)
Man you talked to Freez?

Short Change
Word on the street, that Dee Strong and Snap went at it last night!

Creem
Damn, the game starts in fifteen minutes and we can't do nothing without Freez. I think we should go look for him.

PARKING LOT:

Smoov, Creem and Short Change are walking toward the jeep.

Smoov
(to Short Change)
Anybody get hurt?

Short Change doesn't hear him and doesn't respond. Smoov grabs Short Change by the arm.

Smoov
Did anybody get hurt?

Short Change
Damn man! They got away!

They get in the jeep and Creem cranks up. As they're pulling out, Smoov picks up the car phone and tries to call Freez. Freez drives up before they can pull away. He pulls up beside the jeep.

Short Change
Where you been man?

Freez
Short, I ain't for that shit today!

Creem re-parks the jeep and cuts off. They get out of the jeep and Freez gets out of the car. Smoov and Creem walk over to meet Freez.

> Smoov
> Freez, we were worried about you!

> Creem
> Yeah man, you had us freaked out!

> Freez
> (smilingly)
> You niggas sound like the Harlem boy's choir.
> Damn!

> Short Change
> Stupid motherfucker, we were worried!

> Freez
> Well, as you can see, ain't shit wrong with me!
> So, can we go play ball?

> Smoov
> Let's do it!

They head for the court.

SIDELINE OF COURT:

Smoov, Creem and Freez are gearing up for play when Mr. Eddie walks up to them with a clipboard in hand.

> Mr. Eddie
> Hey fellas, you guys won't be playing The
> Syndicate Boyz today. Somebody messed up
> on the schedule! You'll be playing The Bronx
> Hoopers.

BASKETBALL COURT:

Three Deep is playing the Bronx Hoopers. The Hoopers are a pretty good team and they're playing a close game against Three Deep. Freez isn't playing up to par, but Creem and Smoov are playing exceptionally well to cover for him. Short Change is on the sideline trying to gear up some players for Three Card Marley.

LATER IN THE GAME:

Three Deep is starting to pull away from The Bronx Hoopers.

IN THE STANDS:

Short Change is playing Three Card Marley on the bleacher seats.

> Short Change
> (shuffling the cards)

Now you see em, now you don't! Keep your eyes on the card you want! Are you looking for the Ace? Can you see it now? You gonna lose your money anyhow!

COURT:

As the game is nearing the end, Mr. Eddie looks into the stands and sees Short Change. He continues to officiate the game.

WINNER'S BOARD:

Three Deep moves up on the winner's board.

SIDELINES: AFTER GAME

Short Change is congratulating Three Deep as they walk off the court.

> Short Change
> Man y'all kicked ass! But, damn Freez you was lackin'!

> Freez
> I know Gee! I couldn't get off! I got a lot on my damn mind.

> Smoov
> Don't trip dude. Everything's going alright.

Mr. Eddie walks up.

> Mr. Eddie
> (to Short Change)
> Come here! (he grabs Short Change by the arm).

> Short Change
> (surprised)
> What's up with that Mr. Eddie!

> Mr. Eddie
> I warned you! I told you no more gambling in my park. But you ignored it! Don't bring your ass back here no more during this tournament!

> Short Change
> What did I do, Mr. Eddie?

> Mr. Eddie
> I was watching you all during the game, in the bleachers playing cards and taking people's

money! Now, I want you out of the park! And
don't come back!

Mr. Eddie turns and walks away.

> Smoov
> Man, when are you going to learn?

> Short Change
> I didn't do nothin'!

> Creem
> That's bullshit! I saw you too!

Smoov's family walks up to congratulate them.

> Mr. Starling
> Good game boys! Freez what's wrong son?

> Freez
> Aah, nothing, Mr. Starling. I'm straight!

> Mr. Starling
> Alright. We're having a few friends over a little
> later today. Why don't you guys come over
> and bring a guest if you like!

Mr. Starling and the family walk off in one direction and the boys in the other.

> Freez
> Man, that nigga was quick! He kept getting
> by me!

> Creem
> Yeah, but he couldn't hold you either. That's
> why I kept feeding you in the post!

CUT TO:

FREEZ'S HOUSE: SAME DAY

Freez pulls into his spot and gets out of the car. As he's walking to the house, a
JUNKIE, walks up.

> Junkie
> I know Dee told me not to come here man (he
> sniffles several times) but I gotta see him!

> Freez
> Get the fuck on! Ain't nothin' happenin' here!

The junkie walks off and Freez walks into the house.

INT. HOUSE:

Freez enters the house and stops at the door upon seeing his mother walk into the kitchen. He walks slowly to the kitchen and stands in the door watching her as she washes dishes and cooks. She looks hung over, but she's tried to fix herself up.

>   Freez
> You alright Momma?

>   Nita
>   (at the stove)
> Yeah, I'm fine! I know you're probably hungry.
> I'll be finished cookin' in a minute!

>   Freez
> That's okay. I'm going over to Smoov's house
> for a little get together.

>   Nita
> Boy, I've slavin' in this kitchen all day! You
> gonna eat some of this good ole' home stuff!
> So, go on in there and clean up! So, go on in
> there and clean up! The food'll be done in five
> minutes!

Freez smiles and walks off toward the bedroom. **FOLLOW** as he enters the bedroom. Dee Strong is lying in bed asleep. He doesn't wake up when Freez enters the room. Freez stands and stares at Dee Strong for a moment. He turns and walks out of the room.

>   **CUT TO:**

SMOOV'S HOUSE: THAT EVENING

There are SEVERAL PEOPLE in the living room. Smoov and Mr. Starling are playing a game of cards called **"bid whist"** against **A LADY AND HER HUSBAND.** Short Change is at the grill talking with Mrs. Starling about the food, when Freez and Nikki enter the backyard.

>   Short Change
> What's up Nigga?

>   Freez
> You! And that extra large plate!

>   Short Change
> Nigga, you walk in talkin' shit!

>   Freez
> Where's Smoov?

>   Short Change
> He's over there.

                    Freez
          I'll get with you in a minute.

Freez and Nikki walk over to the card table.

                    Smoov
          It's about time!

                    Freez
          Man, my moms wouldn't let me leave, until I ate
          dinner with her! Has Creem made it yet?

                    Smoov
          Yeah, he's inside.

Nikki starts to ease away as Freez watches the game.

                    Freez
          Who's winning?

                    Smoov
          We killin' em!

KITCHEN:

Creem and Mrs. Starling are in the kitchen. Mrs. Starling is carrying a tray of chicken
out to the grill.

                    Mrs. Starling
          Chris, keep an eye on my baked beans, while I
          go put the chicken on the grill okay sugar?

                    Creem
          Sure Mrs. Starling. No problem.

                    Mrs. Starling
          Thank you baby, I'll be right back!

Mrs. Starling exits outside as Nikki enters the kitchen. They greet each other as they
pass. Nikki stops and looks at Creem who's checking the baked beans. When he
looks up, he sees Nikki.

                    Nikki
          Hi, Creem!

                    Creem
          What's up?

                    Nikki
          You, and,…

Mrs. Starling rushes in the kitchen.

                    Mrs. Starling

> Okay Chris, go ahead and take those Ribs out!
> I'll take care of the beans!

Creem takes a tray of ribs off the counter and walks outside, leaving Nikki standing and watching as he leaves.

BACKYARD:

Creem walks out of the kitchen with the tray of ribs. He takes them over to Mrs. Starling. Freez turns and sees him and walks over to him.

>   Freez
>   (to Creem)
>   What's up, Gee?

>   Creem
>   (shakes Freez's hand)
>   Yo, homey! Looks like you feeling alright!

>   Freez
>   You damn right, I'm feelin' alright!

Mrs. Starling turns around.

>   Mrs. Starling
>   What did you say?

>   Freez
>   Oh, nothing Mrs. Starling.

She smiles and continues tending the grill. Smoov and his father suddenly jump up enthused, having run a **"BOSTON"** on their opponents.

                                                              CUT TO:

HARLEM RUCKERS PARK: NEXT DAY

The Syndicate Boyz watch on as Three Deep dominate their opponent. Freez is playing his best game yet. Freez, Creem and Smoov motivate each other as they play. MUSIC UP as they play Carsello's Amor Mio.

WINNER'S BOARD:

Three Deep moves up on the winner's board.

COURT:

The Syndicate Boyz are playing and beating their opponent as Three Deep looks on.

WINNER'S BOARD:

The Syndicate Boyz move up on the winner's board. There are only two teams left, Three Deep and The Syndicate Boyz!

PARKING LOT: AFTER GAME

Freez, Creem, Smoov and Nikki are walking to the cars. Dee Strong and two of his boys are sitting in a convertible nearby. They blow the horn to get Freez's attention.

> Freez
> Hold up! I'll be right back!

Freez walks over to Dee Strong. The others continue toward the car. When they get to the cars, Smoov sees Short Change standing outside the park area.

> Short Change
> Smoov! Smoov! Come here!

> Smoov
> Let me go see what this lil nigga wants.

Smoov walks off. Creem gets into his jeep. Nikki has sat on the hood of Freez's car, but seeing an opportunity to talk to Creem, she walks over to the jeep.

> Nikki
> Mind if I sit down?

> Creem
> What you want to sit here for?

> Nikki
> To talk.

> Creem
> So, talk.

> Nikki
> If I gave you my phone number, would you use it?

> Creem
> You think you slick, don't you! Who do I look like! Boo, Boo the fool! Why you trying to play me and my boy like two donuts. You kickin' it with Freez! Now you want to get with me! I don't think so! I don't get clown like that!

> Nikki
> You ain't shit, mixed breed!

> Creem
> Neither is your momma!

She turns and walks back over to Freez's car and sits on the hood. Freez walks up and Dee Strong drives by and hollers to Creem.

> Dee Strong

Good game, Gee!

> Creem
> Yeah, man! See you at the championship game, next Saturday!

Freez stops in front on Nikki.

> Freez
> Where's Smoov?

> Nikki
> (gesturing)
> Over there!

Freez opens the car doors and he and Nikki get in. He winds the windows down, cranks the engine and drives over to where Smoov and Short Change are standing. Creem follow in his jeep.

> Freez
> (to Short Change)
> I bet you wished you hadn't fucked up now, don't ya! You missed a damn good game by the Deep Crew!

> Short Change
> Nothin' I ain't seen before fool!

> Freez
> I don't know kid! I throw down a new one today! It was a sick Le Bron James dunk.

> Short Change
> Oh, yeah! Put it on YouTube then! (he laughs) Naw, seriously though dog, I'm starvin' like Marvin! Let's go eat!

> Smoov
> Yeah, I'm down with that!

> Creem
> Me too!

> Freez
> Cool! Let me drop her off and I'll meet y'all at Sylvia's by six o'clock. Come on, Short, you can ride with me, but no gamblin' in the car!

They all laugh, then finally drive off.

CUT TO:

INT. SYLVIA'S KITCHEN: SAME DAY

Freez, Smoov, Creem, and Short Change are sitting at a table talking and eating dinner.

                    Smoov
          Did you hear about Sly Boy! That nigga got
          smoked! Over nothin'!

                    Creem
          What happened!

                    Smoov
          I heard he looked at some dude's lady, the dude
          fronted him, then the next thing you know, BAP!
          BAP! BAP! Three times in the chest!

                    Creem
          That's some fucked up shit! It's senseless!

                    Freez
          It's a way of life! Only the strong survive in the
          ghetto!

                    Short Change
          (concerned more about food)
          Smoov, you gonna eat them greens?

Smoov annoyingly nods his head NO!

                    Short Change
          Thanks, dog! (he scrapes the greens from
          Smoov's plate into his). This shit is good!

                    Freez
          A few months back, I saw a nigga get blasted
          cause he was wearin' the wrong shit! At the
          wrong time! In the wrong place! And as far
          as I'm concerned the nigga deserved what he
          got! He should've known better!

                    Smoov
          Man, listen to what you're saying. Are you
          endorsing black on black crime? That shit's
          wack!

                    Freez
          I didn't say I liked it! But if a nigga tries to do
          me! I'm gonna do him first! Besides! Ain't shit
          we can do about it!

                    Smoov

Bullshit! We made it like this! We can change the shit! We need our brotherhood back! Do you love anybody?

> Freez
> Yeah, I love lots of people!

> Smoov
> Then, that's where we start! With the positive! Diss the negative! We got to wake up and realize that we're not adversaries! We got to improve our way of life for the future of out kids!

There's a moment of complete silence. Then...

> Short Change
> Damn! You sound like a Baptist minister!

CUT TO:

CREEM'S HOUSE: THE NEXT WEEK

Mrs. Starling is at the door, ringing the doorbell. Victoria opens the door.

> Victoria
> Hello, Mrs. Starling. Thanks for coming on such short notice.

She enters the house and Victoria closes the door.

CUT TO:

LIVING ROOM:

Lois Starling sits down.

> Victoria
> Can I get you anything?

> Lois
> No thank you. I'm fine.

> Victoria
> Well, Mrs. Starling I bet you're wondering why I called you here?

> Lois
> Yes.

Victoria sits facing Lois.

> Victoria
> I want to talk to you about our sons!

Lois
What about our sons?

Victoria
I'm sure you already know about this basketball tournament that they're playing in.

Lois
Yes, I do. I've even gone to one of their games. You know they make a very good team.

Victoria
I'm sure they are. I hope my directness doesn't offend you, Mrs. Starling, but I don't approve of my son's choice of friends.

Lois
(slightly offended)
Pardon me! Why is that? What choice of friends?

Victoria
It's not so much your son. I think Steve, which is his name, right?

Lois
Yes! That is his name!

Victoria
I think Steve is a very nice kid! It's the others and the environment they force my son to be in that bothers me!

Lois
I don't think they're forcing Chris to do anything! Chris is there because he wants to be there! As far as Jeff and Alvin are concerned,...

Victoria
Are they the ones called Freez and Short Change or something like that?

Lois
Yes! And they're both good boys! They just need a little guidance!

Victoria
Maybe that's the case, but your son and mine both have a good future ahead of them. And, I don't want Chris' friendship with these boys to interfere with his future. His father and I have

> invested a lot of time and money into seeing that Chris reach certain goals. And, I'm not going to let these boys ruin our lives!

>   Lois
> Mrs. Collins, I think you're over reacting!

Victoria gets up and walks over to a small desk near the window and returns with three checks in her hand.

>   Victoria
> Lois, I'm prepared to pay you hand-somely for your help. And, as you can see I am also prepared to financially compensate the parents of those two boys in trade and with the understanding that they will keep their sons away from mine.

>   Lois
> You're serious, aren't you?

>   Victoria
> If you would take these checks to the boy's parents and explain to them that all I want is my son back with no outside interference, I'll pay you whatever you ask for?

>   Lois
>   (standing)
> Mrs. Collins, its one thing to insult the boys, but truly another to insult me! I'll see myself out. Thank you!

Lois walks out of the living room and out the door. Victoria stands and stares at her as she walks out.

                                                    CUT TO:

EXT. CREEM'S HOUSE:

Creem is driving up as Lois is pulling away. He wonders what she's doing there.

He parks and jumps out of the jeep and enters the house.

INT. LIVING ROOM:

Creem walks into the living room and sees his mother standing at the window, staring out.

>   Creem
> What was Mrs. Starling doing here?

>   Victoria

I invited her over.

Creem
What for?

Victoria
For a mother to mother conversation!

Creem
What have you done, mother?

She turns and stares at Creem momentarily and turns and walks up the stairs. He watches as she disappears up the stairway.

CUT TO:

STREET IN FRONT OF FREEZ'S BUILDING: THAT EVENING

FOCUS on MERCEDES BENZ emblem on the tires of a car pulling up to Freez's house. The car stops and Victoria looks around at her surroundings before slowly exiting the car. She's dressed extremely nice and looks very out of place in the neighborhood. She checks the address on the paper in her hand, then walks slowly up to the house in front of her and knocks on the door. A FEW of the NEIGHBORS, who are out on the block, stare at her. Nita opens the door. She's still slightly sober, having only had a few drinks. She stares at Victoria for a moment.

Nita
Can I help you?

Victoria
May I come in?

Nita
Depends on what you want.

Victoria
I want to talk to you about your son, Freez!

Nita
What about Freez?

Victoria
If you'd let me in, we can discuss it!

Nita moves to the side and Victoria enters the house. Nita closes the door behind her.

INT. HOUSE:

The living room is fairly clean. Victoria stands at the door and Nita stares at her.

Nita
Have a seat!

Victoria walks over to the sofa and sits down. Nita follows her to the sofa.

> **Nita**
> Can I get you something? I ain't got no coffee or nothin' like that! But if you want some beer or wine, I got that!

> **Victoria**
> No thank you. I don't have much time. I just stopped by to talk to you about your son.

Nita sits down facing Victoria.

> **Nita**
> Is he in jail?

> **Victoria**
> I surely hope not! look I'm not a social worker or anything like that! My name Victoria Collins. You may know my son, Chris!

> **Nita**
> Oh, Creem's your boy?

> **Victoria**
> Yes! And the reason I'm here is because I need your help!

> **Nita**
> My help?

> **Victoria**
> Yes, your help. You see, Chris will be graduating soon and then he'll be attending Harvard.

> **Nita**
> What's Harvard?

> **Victoria**
> It's a prestigious University. Lately, Chris hasn't been doing too well in school and I believe it's because of his involve-ment with your son!

> **Nita**
> Fuck you!

> **Victoria**
> No, I don't think you're understanding me!

> **Nita**
> Really! Then straighten me out!

> Victoria
>
> Chris has been spending more time on the basketball courts with your son than he has been studying.

> Nita
>
> My boy, he's a pretty good basketball player too!

> Victoria
>
> Yes, well what I propose in the best interest of both of our sons, is that you keep Freez away from Chris! Now, I'm willing to pay you for your time and effort!

> Nita
>
> You want me to keep my boy away from yours?

> Victoria
>
> That's all! And I'm prepared to pay you $3000 to do so!

> Nita
>
> You're offering me $3,000 to keep Freez away from Creem?

Victoria removes a check from her pocketbook and extends it to Nita, who takes the check and examines it.

> Victoria
>
> All I have to do is fill your name in and the money's yours.

> Nita
>
> And, all I have to do is keep Freez away from Creem?

> Victoria
>
> That's all!

Nita stands and walks around the room contemplating the deal that Victoria has offered. She turns to Victoria.

> Nita
>
> You got any idea how I'm suppose to do that?

> Victoria
>
> No, but I'm sure you'll think of something! Do we have a deal?

> Nita
> (after a moments thought)
> Yeah. We got a deal.

Victoria stands and walks up to Nita and extends her hand for a handshake. Nita shakes her hand and they both smile.

> Nita
> Don't you need to put my name here on this line?

> Victoria
> Yes!

Nita hands her the check and Victoria takes a pen out of her pocket-book. She looks up at Nita.

> Victoria
> What's your full name?

> Nita
> Anita Jamison.

Victoria fills her name in on the check and hands the check back to her.

> Victoria
> I must be going now, Anita, but its been nice meeting you.

> Nita
> Yeah, sure.

Victoria starts toward the door and then turns around to Nita.

> Victoria
> If you should have any problems cashing the check, just call me. My phone number's on the check.

> Nita
> I will.

Victoria walks out the door.

EXT. HOUSE:

Victoria exits the house and walks to her car. She unlocks the door and gets in. As she's driving off, Freez drives up. He stops in the middle of the street, shocked at seeing Victoria at his house. He speeds into the driveway and jumps out of the car and runs into the house.

INT: HOUSE

Freez enters the house. He stops in the living room.

> Freez
>
> Momma! Momma!

Nita walks out of her room and into the living room. She stops at the edge of the hallway and stares at Freez.

> Freez
>
> What was Mrs. Collins doing here?

> Nita
>
> She was looking for Creem?

> Freez
>
> Looking for Creem? Why would she come here looking for Creem?

> Nita
>
> I guess she thought he might be here, I don't know!

> Freez
>
> She wouldn't come here just to look for him. She might call, but she ain't gonna drive down here.

> Nita
>
> So, what are you trying to say? That I'm lying.

> Freez
>
> I ain't sayin' all that! But, you ain't tellin' it all!

Nita walks over to the coffee table and picks her cigarettes up and lights on. She turns to Freez.

> Nita
>
> I think you should stay from around that boy of her's anyway.

> Freez
>
> Why?

> Nita
>
> Cause I said so! That's why! He ain't good for you to be hangin' with!

> Freez
>
> Since when did you decide who I should be hangin' with?

> Nita
>
> Since I raised you from the time you was born?

> Freez
>
> But raising me doesn't always mean making my decisions because I'm grown and I can decide on what works for my life and my future.

> Nita
>
> Yeah but you makin' decisions don't mean that you always right.

> Freez
>
> But my decisions are based on my friends and who I play ball with. And ballin' is my way of life.

> Nita
>
> I understand what you are sayin' but if you don't start trying to separate yourself from people that might bring you down you will not have a way of life and a way to play ball.

> Freez
>
> I know Creem, Smoov, Short Change and everybody else that I kick it with and its all good.

> Nita
>
> It's only good because you don't want to see the bigger picture because you are always caught up in the moment and the hype.

Freez looks over to the coffee table and glances on the check placed earlier by Nita. He grabs the check and confronts his mother in anger.

> Freez
>
> What the hell is this? So, this is why you're giving me all of this quick talk about stayin' away from Creem. You think you can take my friendship away based on this check.

> Nita
>
> I'm not trying to take away your friendship. I'm just lookin' out for your future.

Freez walks over to the phone and starts to dial Creem.

> Nita
>
> Who you callin'? Freez, I know you hear me talkin' to you!

He doesn't answer her. When Creem answers the phone.

                            Freez
            Yo man, your moms done paid my moms $3,000
            to separate us!

INTERCUT:

CREEM'S BEDROOM:

Creem is lying on the bed talking on his BlackBerry. He sits up attentively when
Freez tells him about Victoria's visit to his house.

                            Creem
            She wouldn't do that!

                            Freez
            Bullshit! She just left here! and, I got the check
            right here in my hand to prove it! $3,000!

                            Nita
            You hang up that phone! (she tries to snatch
            the phone away from Freez, but isn't able to)
            Hang it up!

                            Creem
            I'll be right over!

FREEZ'S LIVING ROOM:

Freez hangs up the phone and Nita stands staring angrily at him.

                            Nita
            Give me my check!

                            Freez
            I ain't givin' shit!

                            Nita
            You give it to me! Or I'm callin' the police right
            now!

Freez walks into his room and locks the door. Nita follow pulling on the door know
and beating the door.

                            Nita
            Open this door! Open this damn door! I said
            open it!

INT. BEDROOM:

Freez is lying in the top bunk staring at the check. Nita is still screaming and
pounding on the door from the other side.

                                                            CUT TO:

INT. SNAP'S HOUSE – LIVING ROOM: SAME DAY

Snap is sitting on the coach with four of his gang members as they are polishing their guns.

> Snap
>
> I don't give a fuck on how long it takes. I'm gonna blow that nigga, Dee Strong, ass away.

> Gang member #1
>
> Were gonna put a cap in his ass.

> Snap
>
> I'm gonna put more than a cap in his ass. I'm gonna unload every bullet that I have until he is done.

> Gang member #2
>
> You know you can try to catch that nigga at the basketball courts.

> Gang member #3
>
> And it doesn't matter who he is with. He be rollin' when some weak ass nigga's anyway who ain't even all of that.

> Snap
>
> I don't give a shit if he was rollin' with an army. That nigga took my loot and his punk ass ain't getting' away with that shit.

> Gang member #4
>
> Let's load up our shit and bounce and roll up on that nigga again. This time we ain't gonna miss.

> Snap
>
> I've been waitin' a long time to try to catch somebody to take my frustration out on for all this bullshit I gots to deal with to make it in Harlem.

EXT. SNAP'S BUILDING – SAME DAY

Snap and his gang tucking guns into their jackets as the walk to their cars preparing to cruise around and look for Dee Strong.

> Snap
>
> You nigga's make sure you keep looking out in every direction until we roll up on Dee. If we get a chance to grab him while he is still living, I'm gonna make sure he dies a slow death with bullets all through his ass.

                    Gang #3
        Take a left on the next block 'cause that is
        where he be hangin' and I think there might
        be a bunch of people around.

                    Snap
        Punk ass! Ain't no motherfuckin' civilians!

                                                    CUT TO:

EXT. FREEZ'S HOUSE: SAME NIGHT

Creem is driving up. Freez walks out of the house just as Creem pulls into the drive
way. Freez has the check in his hand. Creem gets out of the jeep and Freez walks
to meet him. He extends the check.

                    Freez
        See this shit! I told you! Your moms don't like
        me!

                    Creem
        Man, I know. I was just frontin' for her all the
        time. But who gives a damn! As far as I'm con-
        cerned we're friends to the end! Damn! I can't
        believe she went this far, though!

                    Freez
        That bitch didn't have no business coming here
        in the first place!

                    Creem
        Bitch? Did you call my mother a bitch? Your
        mom's a bitch! She didn't have any business
        taking the check, with her poor ass in the first
        place!

Freez hits Creem and they start fighting. As they're fighting, they fall to the ground.
During their scuffle, Creem glances and sees **SNAP'S CAR** driving by slowly. Freez
doesn't see at first. Snap and one of his boys are hanging out the window with guns.
(SLOW MOTION) Creem yells.

                    Creem
            It's Snap! Snap!

Freez looks and sees them approaching. They both scramble to get up and run
towards the house. Snap and his boys start shooting. Freez dives to the ground
beside the porch and Creem is hit by a bullet trying to jump on the porch. The
windows of the house shatter! Snap and his boys laugh out and speed away! Freez
gets up off the ground and hurries over to Creem!

                    Freez

> Aah man! Damn! Creem! Creem! Aah fuck!
> Somebody help me! Please!

Several **NEIGHBORS** run out of the house.

> Freez
> Somebody, please call an ambulance! (Freez
> is crying now) Lay still man! You gonna be
> alright!

Freez runs into the house as a neighbor comforts Creem

> Freez
> Momma! Momma! Creem's been shot! Momma!
> Where are you?

Freez runs to the phone and picks the phone up. He dials 911 and turns toward the window. FOCUS on his **POV**, when he sees his mother lying on the floor by the window, shot!

> Freez
> Momma! (echo)

CUT TO:

FREEZ'S HOUSE: SAME NIGHT

Dee Strong drives up in a hurry. There are a **FEW PEOPLE** standing around the building. He drives up and hurries out of the car. He sees Creem lying there being tended to. He runs into the house.

INT. HOUSE:

Dee Strong enters the house. He stops in the doorway.

> Dee Strong
> Freez! Freez! Where you at? Where's
> momma?

Dee Strong finally sees Freez helping their mother who has been shot in the arm. He rushes over to help too.

CUT TO:

EXT. FREEZ'S HOUSE: SAME NIGHT

Paramedics have placed Creem in the ambulance. They turn on their sirens and rush off into the night.

CUT TO:

INT. FREEZ'S HOUSE: SAME NIGHT

Another paramedic unit finally attends to Nita. Freez and Dee Strong are shocked!

CUT TO:

INT. EMERGENCY ROOM OF HOSPITAL:

FOCUS on **DOUBLE DOOR** as an **EMT CREW** rush through the door with Creem on a stretcher. They rush down the hallway and turn into a room.

HALLWAY OF HOSPITAL:

Jonathan and Victoria Collins rush into the hallway and up to the nurse's station, where **SEVERAL NURSES** are working. Victoria is extremely upset.

> Jonathan
> Excuse me! We're Mr. and Mrs. Jonathan Collins! We were told that our son, Chris Collins was brought here!

> Nurse
> Yes sir, he was!

> Jonathan
> Can you tell us how he is?

> Nurse
> I don't have any information now sir, except that he had been shot! I won't have any more information until Dr. Richards comes out of emergency.

DR. RICHARDS is walking up. The nurse sees him.

> Nurse
> Here comes Dr. Richards now.

Mr. and Mrs. Collins turn around to meet Dr. Richards.

> Jonathan
> We're Chris Collins' parents! How is our son?

> Dr. Richards
> For the moment, he's stable. But he's lost a lot of blood and we're going to have to operate to remove the bullet. As best as we can tell the bullet is lodge near his spinal tap and there's a possibility of paralysis.

Victoria breaks down and cries. Jonathan comforts her.

> Dr. Richards
> We're preparing him for surgery, but we'll need you to sign some release forms first.

> Jonathan

Alright!

Dr. Richards walks off and Jonathan stands trying to comfort his wife.

CUT TO:

EXT. FREEZ'S HOUSE:

Dee strong pulls into the driveway with Freez in the passenger seat. As the car comes to a stop, Freez jumps out in a hurry and rushes into the house. Dee Strong quickly follows.

INT. HOUSE:

Freez runs into the house and straight to his bedroom. Dee Strong follows.

BEDROOM:

Freez has one of Dee Strong's pistols loading it. Dee Strong runs up to Freez and snatches the gun, but Freez won't let go.

> Dee Strong
> Give me this motherfuckin' gun!

> Freez
> I ain't giving you shit! Get the fuck outta my way!

> Dee Strong
> So, you all that nigga! What you gonna do! Fuck me up! Go ahead pull the trigger! Pull it! Punk ass nigga, put the gun down!

> Freez
> Move!

Dee Strong slaps Freez, knocking him to the floor. Dee Strong has the pistol in his hand and he stands staring at Freez.

> Dee Strong
> If you get your ass up off that floor, I'm gonna fuck you up!

Freez attempts to get up and Dee Strong knocks him back to the floor.

> Freez
> (crying)
> You bitch!

Freez tries to get up again and Dee Strong knocks him down again!

> Dee Strong
> Look at me nigga!

Freez turns away from Dee Strong. Dee Strong grabs him and makes him look at him.

> Dee Strong
> I said look at me! Take a good look! What you see! I'll tell you! Twenty-six years of pure hell! That's what you see! Don't worry about Snap, mother-fuckin' ass! That's my problem! You just keep your ass in bounds.

DISSOLVE TO:

FREEZ'S LIVING ROOM: TWO DAYS LATER

Freez is lying on the sofa staring blankly at the ceiling, when Smoov and Short Change knock on the door. Freez doesn't answer.

> Short Change
> (from outside)
> Freez! It's us man! Open the door! Open the motherfuckin' door! We know you in thee!

> Smoov
> Come on man! Let us in!

They're silent outside for a moment. Finally the door opens slowly. Smoov and Short Change walk inside. Freez moves to the side as the boys walk past him. Smoov looks around the living room (HIS POV) this is cluttered. The place is a wreck throughout. Freez walks back to the sofa and sits down. He's very distant.

> Smoov
> Man you need to clean this place up! Your mom's coming home tomorrow!

Smoov starts picking things up. Short Change is standing watching him.

> Smoov
> What you watching me for? Pick the ironing board up off the floor!

> Short Change
> Damn Smoov! What you checkin' me for?

Short Change picks the ironing board up.

LIVING ROOM: LATER

The boys have cleaned the house up and they're all sitting in the living room. Freez still appears to be distant.

> Smoov
> (to Freez)

Look man. I know you bothered. But everything's going to be fine. Your mom's gonna be home tomorrow and Creem's much better. Both of them are gonna need you. You know!

Short Change
We're in your corner dude.

Freez
(looking up slowly)
Yeah, I know B. but a lot of shit is on my mind and its hard to focus on everything and everyone that's involved in my life including you, Smoov, Creem and my family.

Smoov
You gotta realize that everything happens for a reason and you gotta continue to believe in yourself and pull it all together.

Freez
Don't start giving me some gangsta preaching bullshit. I know you're not all the way down, but you got dirt too.

Smoov
Yeah, but I don't give up on my family and friends when something goes down.

Freez
You be talkin' a lot of shit but some of the shit you say makes sense. You just be sayin' it in a twisted way. I understand where you coming from, I'm just dealin' with the reality of my life and the small amount of people that are supportive of my dreams and goals. Life is not easy in Harlem.

Smoov
Look, your nigga Creem might be hurt but that don't mean that we gotta throw in the towel. We got mad skills and eventually if all of us get our act together and all the bullshit around here would stop we might have a chance to do something with our talent playing ball and get paid with a ticket out of here.

Freez

Yeah, what about if Creem don't get better. He could be paralyzed or some crazy shit could happen while he is at the hospital. That nigga took a bullet because we were all down together. You know Creem don't even have to be fuckin' with us 'cause his family comes from real money.

                Short Change
Creem always been keepin' it real with us. No matter what goes down with Creem, we are all brothers to the end.

                Freez
I got to find out from Ms. Collins what's goin' on with Creem and how he's comin' along.

                Short Change
Yeah, you never know, that nigga might not be hurt that bad. Let's just pray and stay positive.

                Freez
Yeah, but, if he isn't hurt that bad how do we know he still wants to be down to play in the tournament.

                Short Change
We don't know unless we find out what the fuck is goin' on. So let's get off our ass and try to make somethin' happen.

                Freez
We need to find out if the tournament can be postponed or delayed.

                Short Change
Nigga please, this ain't the NBA finals and you'll nigga sure ain't Kobe or Le Bron.

                Freez
Shut the fuck up and let's find out if we can get in contact with Mr. Eddie.

                Short Change
I hate that bitch ass nigga. He ain't gonna let you change anything that has been scheduled for the tournament because this is his shit.

                Freez

Why you have this fucked up attitude with Mr. Eddie. He's always been alright with us from day 1 and he has seen us grow up so he knows what we are really about, you just can't gamble in his park.

Short Change
Well actually I bumped into Mr. Eddie and he seemed to have a fucked up attitude towards me but it could have been because he sounded disappointed because he has been hearing all the negative shit that's been goin' on in the streets.

Freez
What else did he say and when did you meet with him?

Short Change
I didn't say I met with the nigga. I bumped into him a couple days ago but he told you guys are out if Creem can't play. I asked him if I could take his place.

Freez
What the fuck, nigga, why didn't you tell me about this shit.

Short Change
Damn! I forgot! And he said no to me anyway.

Freez
That's fucked up!

Short Change
Freez, I know you can talk Mr. Eddie into changing his mind!

Freez
Naw man! He meant that shit! We ain't in.

Short Change
Man, I know he'll change his mind for you! Come on?

Freez
Come on. Let's bounce and try to see what's up with Creem first.

CREEM'S ROOM: LATER

The boys have gone to the hospital to see Creem and let him know what is up. The boys are preparing to leave his room. They're walking out the door. Freez turns around to Creem. He does the Three Deep sign. Creem smiles. They exit.

HALLWAY NEAR CREEM'S ROOM:

The boys are walking down the hallway.

> SHORT CHANGE
> I think you should go talk to Mr. Eddie now about me playing in Creems spot!

> Freez
> No man. I think we should wait and bust it on him just before the game! With everybody there, it'll be hard for him to say no!

> Short Change
> Yeah, you're right! That's a smart move!

Victoria turns into the hallway. They stop talking and stare ahead as though they were staring through her. As they pass,... each other nothing is said. She stops and looks back at them and they continue on.

> Short Change
> Did I tell you that Bitch came by my house too! Me and my old man took that money and spent the hell out of it and I'm still gonna be friends with Creem!

CUT TO:

HARLEM RUCKERS PARK: NEXT MORNING

The park is crowded and cars are still driving in from everywhere- Philly, NJ, and etc.-. **PAN** the area. Smoov and Freez are walking toward Mr. Eddie who's standing at the sign in table.

> Smoov
> So what you gonna say?

> Freez
> What you mean, what am I gonna say? Nigga, you beggin' too!

They walk up to Mr. Eddie. When he sees them he pulls them to the side.

> Mr. Eddie
> Freez, I'm sorry about what happened!

> Freez
> Thanks. She's doing much better now. And Creem's coming along too.

                    Mr. Eddie
Now, what are you going to do about the game?
You got somebody to fill in?

                    Freez
Yeah! Short Change!

                    Mr. Eddie
No! No way!

                    Freez
Come on Mr. Eddie! We've come to far to have
you take it away from us! What Short did was
wrong we all know that! But everybody makes
mistakes! Let him play! It won't happen again,
I promise!

                    Mr. Eddie
Freez, I understand! Believe me! But , he
brought this on himself and now it's hurting
your team! If you can't find someone else, you
have to forfeit the game!

Victoria has overheard the conversation and walks up to Mr. Eddie and the boys.
They're shocked to see her.

                    Victoria
Excuse me. Mr. Eddie, Hi. I'm Mrs. Collins.
Creems mother.

                    Mr. Eddie
Yes! I know your husband Jonathan very well!
I'm sorry about Creem.

                    Victoria
Thank you. I overheard that the boys may have
to forfeit this game. I hope you'll reconsider as
these boys have worked extremely hard to get
to the championship. And it isn't any fault of
theirs that my son can't play. Therefore, I think
Short Change should be allowed to play.

                    Mr. Eddie
I guess you're right. (he looks at Smoov and
Freez) Go get Short Change and gear up! The
game starts in twenty-five minutes!

The boys thank Victoria and she smiles and walks to the stands and sits down. The
boys hurry to the sidelines.

COURT: LATER

A TRIO OF GIRLS are singing the National Anthem. They sing it soulfully.

ON THE COURT:

The two teams are set for the tip off. Mr. Eddie starts the game. Both teams are playing to their potential. The Syndicate Boyz get the ball and dribble up court where they score. Immediately, the crowd is totally into the game as both teams show off their playing abilities. Everyone is surprised to see Short Change display some basketball talent. Mr. Eddie calls a close call on Short Change.

> Short Change
> Foul! That wasn't no foul!

> Mr. Eddie
> I said it was a foul!

> Short Change
> That's a bullshit call!

The fans boo the call too. Freez and Smoov walk up to Short Change who's pissed off.

> Freez
> Chill out man before you get tossed!

> Short Change
> But man, it wasn't no foul!

> Freez
> I know! But Chill! We gonna win!

They resume play. Freez makes a three pointer and Nikki jumps up and down in the stands. Victoria is really into the game. As we **PAN THE STANDS WE SEE** Freez's mother just arriving with her arm bandaged up.

CUT TO:

NEIGHBORHOOD STREET: SAME MORNING

Dee Strong and two of his boys cruise the streets. They stop at a stoplight and a young boy runs up to the car.

> Boy
> I just saw Snap!

> Dee Strong
> Where?

> Boy
> Over on 145th St. and St. Nick.

Dee Strong pulls off.

CUT TO:

HARLEM RUCKERS PARK:

The game between Three Deep and The Syndicate Boyz is still being played. The Syndicate Boyz are winning, but it's a close game. The game is 51–50. Freez flies through the air for a one hand slam dunk only to have it rejected by his cocky opponent. Hyped, the defender talks a lot of trash to Freez, calling him all sorts of nasty names to the point that Freez pushes him. A technical foul is called and the opponent goes to the free throw line where he misses the crucial shot.

                                                                        CUT TO:

HARLEM STREET:

Dee Strong and his boys are parked down the street from the crack-house run by Snap.

                         Snoopy
                 What we gonna do Dee?

                        Dee Strong
         We gonna sit here and wait for that motherfucker
         to come out!

                         Snoopy
                 That might be all day!

                        Dee Strong
         Motherfucker, you got something else to do?

                         Snoopy
                 Naw, man! I'm just sayin'!

                        Dee Strong
         Don't say shit! Just sit there and relax!

Dee Strong fumbles the gun he's holding and stares at the house, anticipating Snap's exit.

                                                                        CUT TO:

HARLEM RUCKERS PARK:

One of The Syndicate Boyz takes a long jump shot and misses. Smoov grabs the rebound and calls time-out! With 12 seconds left in the game Freez comes up with a plan.

                          Freez
             Man, we down by two points. We can tie this
             bitch up!

Taking to the court again Freez talks to himself. As he stares at his opponent, he reaches down and tightly ties his sneakers. When the whistle blows, Smoov tosses the ball in bounds to Short Change who attempts a pass to Freez that is blocked. Short

Change gets the ball back and goes for a jumper with seconds left. He makes it and ties the game. They are excited.

CUT TO:

HARLEM STREET:

Snap ant three of his boys exit the house. Dee Strong cranks the car and as Snap walks onto the sidewalk he pulls off toward them. He and his boys start shooting. They shoot one of the guys, but Snap runs and manages to make it down an alley. Dee Strong jumps out of the car and chases behind him.

CUT TO:

HARLEM RUCKERS PARK:

Both teams are on the sideline. The SCOREBOARD shows the score. 71-71. Mr. Eddie is talking through a megaphone from center court.

> Mr. Eddie
> With both teams tied at 71 all, we'll have a five
> minute overtime period.

Mr. Eddie walks off the court. Smoov, Freez, and Short Change are sitting on the sideline.

> Short Change
> Man, these motherfuckers are pretty good!
> But, Mr. Eddie given em some calls too!

> Smoov
> Man, he's just doing his job!

> Freez
> Besides, if it wasn't for Creem's old lady, we
> wouldn't be playin'!

> Short Change
> Yeah, you right!

> Freez
> So let's win this motherfucker!

They walk back onto the court and start practicing.

CUT TO:

ALLEY:

Snap is running through the alley. He's been shot in the arm and is holding it close to his body. Dee Strong is running behind him. Dee Strong shoots at him and misses. Snap manages to climb over a wall and continue running. Dee Strong climbs the wall and continues behind him.

CUT TO:

HARLEM RUCKERS PARK:

The overtime play has begun and both teams are playing good ball. When one team makes a point, the other counters and scores. Mr. Eddie calls another foul on Short Change. Short Change can't believe the call and just stares at Mr. Eddie. So do Smoov and Freez, as they didn't think it was a foul either. They finally resume play.

CUT TO:

NEIGHBORHOOD STREET:

Snap is running down a street and Dee Strong is running behind him, shooting at him. The **PEOPLE** that are on the street scatter.

CUT TO:

HARLEM RUCKERS PARK:

There are only a few seconds left on the clock and The Syndicate Boyz are winning by one point. Smoov has called time out.

Freez

Get me the ball! I'm gonna kill this
motherfucker!

They resume play. Smoov passes the ball to Short Change and he launches an ollie-oop pass to the basket.

CUT TO:

NEIGHBORHOOD STREET:

Snap is running from Dee Strong. He manages to get his gun out of his pants and turns toward Dee Strong. Dee Strong already is aimed and shoots him several times in the chest.

SIMULTANEOUSLY:

HARLEM RUCKERS PARK:

Freez leaps toward the basket as the ball reaches the basket. One of The Syndicate Boyz tries to go up and block the shot. Freez spectacularly turns his body in mid-air and throws down a strong reverse slam dunk! Freez hangs on the rim for a moment excited. He finally drops to the ground. Ecstatic, kids spill onto the court smothering Freez and his teammates.

CUT TO:

NEIGHBORHOOD:

Snap lies dead with a sheet pulled over his bloody body. The police have Dee Strong in custody in the police car. The car pulls away.

DISSOLVE TO:

HARLEM RUCKERS PARK:

Freez, Smoov, and Short Change hold their shiny trophy high over their heads in total jubilation. Victoria, Nita and Nikki look on, as does Smoov's family.

CUT TO:

HOSPITAL CORRIDOR:

AS THE CAMERA moves down the corridor, chanting is heard.

Chanting
Three Deep! Three Deep! Three Deep!

The **CAMERA NEARS CREEM'2S ROOM** and enters:

Freez, Smoov, Short Change and Creem are chanting Three Deep. Victoria and Jonathan look on smiling.

DISSOLVE TO:

GRAFFITI COVERED WALL: NYC NIGHT

A YOUNG MAN stands at the wall spray painting around the Three Deep that's already painted on the wall. He paints, "Its Not A Game, Its A Way of Life". **A HELICOPTER'S LIGHT** shines on the wall.

CREDITS ROLL OVER NYC SKYLINE.

THE END

About the Author

With a natural gift and a passion for writing and performing music, Lance Carsello, also known as "DILEMA", has entered into the film and Rock world by storm. He aims to become the voice for young America, as he incorporates his background and life experiences into his music and films. A multi-cultural background of Italian, Hispanic and African-American descent results in having an understanding of mixed relationships and diverse backgrounds of different people and this has helped him to create a realistic and distinctive writing style. "I use my past experiences in life to create stories that will make a difference and have a positive influence for young America."

Carsello was born in the Bronx, New York. At the age of eleven he moved to Texas with his mother. In 1993 he began his career as a songwriter with EMI Music Publishing in NYC. After several years he realized the need to pursue his career as an artist in music and film. Carsello felt that the true meaning of his music was lost when performed by other musicians and believed that he was the only one who could express the real emotion contained within his lyrics. Later on, he decided to combine his love for songwriting and turn his numerous song ideas into screenplays.

Carsello's understanding of film making, from pre-production to post production, progressed through his professional experience within the music industry and the filming of his own videos as a producer and director. He has released Crime For

Loving A Model the album with 10 tracks written, produced and performed by DILEMA himself which was created to cross promote his book "Crime For Loving A Model". It seems Carsello learned how to cross market and promote himself when he was represented as a Rock artist by the celebrity publicist Lizzie Grubman and her PowerGirls which handled the P.R. for his DILEMA Rock Star album.

Carsello, a native New Yorker who lives on the upper east side of Manhattan, already has offers from Hollywood to turn "That Depends On You" and "Crime For Loving A Model" into theatrical big screen successes. If other convicted celebrities can turn their tragedy into triumph, why can't Carsello benefit from his own books, movies and recordings to get out of his "DILEMA" as a "Crime For Loving A Model"? I guess that he can, but "That Depends On You"!

Read more about DILEMA and his projects on www.DilemaRockStar.com.

LANCE CARSELLO IS A WRITER PROUCER AND A DIRECTOR THAT HAS BEEN IN THE FILM AND MUSIC INDUSTRY FOR OVER 20 YEARS. CARSELLO IS ALSO A RECORDING ARTIST CALLED "DILEMA" THAT HAS RECORED OVER 25 ALBUMS BETWEEN THE SOUNDS OF HIP HOP, LATIN, AND ROCK MUSIC.

**Current books published by the
author Lance Carsello**

That Depends On You
Last Shot Basketball
Crime for Loving a Model
Hamptons 21
All Alone

**Titles that are coming soon from
the author Lance Carsello**

Convicted Felon
The Polo Kid
Journals of a RockStar
Urban Salsa The Movie
Triple Threat
Designer Fashion Hotel
Carsello Cartoon Network
Fashion News Network